INTERBEING

by Soraya Bakhbakhi

QUILLKEEPERS PRESS

Copyright © Soraya Bakhbakhi, 2026

Book Cover Image by Soraya Bakhbakhi

Cover Format by Quillkeepers Press

Edit by Stephanie Lamb

All rights reserved. No part of this book may be reproduced in any form or by any electronic or mechanical means, including information storage and retrieval systems, without the permission in writing from the publisher, except by a reviewer who may quote brief passages in a review.

This compilation contains some works of fiction. Locales and public names are sometimes used for atmospheric purposes. Any resemblance to actual people, living or dead, or to businesses, companies, events, institutions, or locales are completely coincidental. Any references to pop culture are owned by their specific companies and are not the property of the author.

There are some poems here within that represent thoughts of the author. Any resemblance to actual events, locals, or persons, living or dead, is entirely coincidental.

ISBN:978-1-969601-02-6

Published by Quillkeepers Press, LLC

PO Box 10236

Casa Grande, AZ 85130

"We are all walking each other home."

— *Ram Dass*

These poems are the sum of many influences and contributions, both of this plane and beyond, for which I am eternally grateful. I am especially thankful for my parents, siblings, darling furbies, wider family, friends both visible and unseen, beloved musicians and writers, failed romances, Portishead seafront, and my secondary school English teachers.

Our interconnectedness is what I strived to express in this chapbook, which I hope you enjoy.

Dedicated to All That Is

Featured Poems

Jiminy Speaks	11
I Took Jiminy's Advice	12
Amnesty	13
All Things Still Pass	14
Be Here Now	15
Clair de Lune	16
For Sooty and Willy	17
Not Plenty of Fish	18
Karuna	19
Ode to Kimberly of Perth	20
Panic Attack in the Hallway	21
Negative Capability	22
Communion	23
Aslama	24
Cactus	25
Finding Grace	26
Sunyata	27
3am	28
A Postcard from Willy	29
The Matrix is Glitching	30
The Sea of Samsara	31
Everything Serves	32

E.B.	33
Ice Cream with my Departed Granddad	34
Interbeing	35
Gnosis	36
Mosaic of Life	37
Ouroboros	38

I stood over potted plants and watered them triumphantly,

my nightdress wafting in the warming air,

feeling I had performed a kind deed; till I rationed the last drops

onto pots coddling sprouted weeds, some tall –

with wild leaves and daring dandelions.

Tired, I made my apologies and vowed to return

the next day with a brimming watering can,

then contemplated removing and replacing them with

perfectly formed roses and dahlias;

I would tidy the area and make it beautiful.

And as I scolded myself for having greasy hair

a soft, disembodied voice whispered,

Love everything anyway.

Jiminy Speaks

Inspired by Bill Hicks, Ram Dass, and my green-fingered elders

I decided to bare my dry, flaking legs

and swollen feet near the sea

unshaved

and let them feel worthy of midsummer sun.

I Took Jiminy's Advice

We bear an invisible knife

held within & pointed without/

if you want to forgive

come to know yourself

then move the blade aside/

to see a shared wound.

Amnesty

You are the wind & tree

its rustling leaves

& loosening soil

wind calms once it has

consumed what nourishes

turmoil & so

you are also the stilling tree

its silencing leaves

& soil clinging to roots in repose.

All Things Still Pass

Dedicated to George Harrison, Timothy Leary, and Lao Tzu

On days like today, when words

seldom adjoin to thought,

the answer to *why all this?*

is clearly

to feel tender breeze

balm flushed cheeks.

Be Here Now

The Moon is least luminous when unseen

as it crosses the horizon's liminal strip

its brow crowning above greening hedges

till solemnly admired from a quiet spring garden

its mournful paper face, lit by love.

Clair de Lune

One of grief's gifts

is to watch death fail;

to parse a veil

through which I slip my love —

                        knowing you can reach.

                        For Sooty and Willy

I cast my line out to the man crafting
heart-shaped sculptures on the shore

He released the bait
preoccupied with making someone else's day

Dejected, I wandered to the memorial bench
behind me

Roy's plaque reads, *Keep smiling.*

Not Plenty of Fish

Dedicated to Roy F. and Mary Oliver

Even waste has a narrative,

& the urine of which I smell

wants to be read like poetry;

with curiosity and compassion.

Karuna

Dedicated to Thich Nhat Hanh

I expect you're now far away

like the bush beyond the

stone wall before me

bulbed with a billion buds

the shade of summer sun

as they do, you share your light

expecting no return.

Ode to Kimberly of Perth

I can't hold onto anything

as though nothing can be owned

& everything wants to be free.

Panic Attack in the Hallway

I gulped the fog and feared
the distance of Grace

nearby, plumes of wildflower
border earl grey sea

they bunch as violet bouquets
held by hidden brides

betrothed to the Mystery

Negative Capability

Mallards glide along glimmering marle

soft sun butters their silhouettes

& sinks into mouth of mountain

the pudding gathers on a pew —

rind showers from the horizon's belch

an amber-lilac swatch swirls on the tide

Communion

If you think you are the authority of your life

try stopping wind from displacing your hair

or to not be at the mercy of another's good or bad day

or altering the course of an earthbound asteroid

or asking the Sun not to eat us in a few billion years

or petitioning a dictator not to drop the bomb

or demanding rainfall over droughted lands

or stopping your parents' ugly divorce

or mending a heart as it breaks

or insisting a loved one not have cancer

or convincing your body not to die.

Aslama

Dedicated to my paternal relatives

I am not so tough/I need:

rare clouds to water the desert &

kind winds to soothe my needled body.

Cactus

The woman behind the table offered me
a carrot,
I put it in a large carrier
& opened the bag the day after —
it had decomposed
orange mush spattered the inside.
I asked myself, *why did she offer this?*
and before the wretch of
resentment howled from my stomach,
I realised she must be a very hopeful person,
who, like most, wants to keep
something fragile alive.

Finding Grace

A mountain is shaped as much by vacant sky

as it is by contours of the land

Sunyata

You went under earlier, then leapt into my lap

& billowed your breath over my face

to reveal *God Is! God Is! God Is!*.

3am

Dedicated to my beloved Sooty

I hadn't heard from you awhile

& asked the astral switchboard for an update:

Do they give cat treats in the afterlife?

Have you settled in or are already reborn?

As I roused from sleep, you appeared

as close as a mime's hands to air

your black paws printed lightly over grey,

adjacent to a dancing ukulele—

then faded.

A Postcard from Willy

Dedicated to my darling Willy

dashes score the lake

flickering and quickening

resembling static

The Matrix is Glitching

I contemplate death

as something abstract

with a faraway gaze

as if scrying into the future

                          of a distant world

meanwhile drooping roses

in a Frida Kahlo vase

weep dry petals

onto the kitchen table

The Sea of Samsara

I drove past a pigeon's remains earlier

& wept.

Across the road, a grey and white feather

landed at the feet of a man

kicked up by coastal wind, as if

guided by God's hand

to bless another's day.

Everything Serves

Isn't it funny what sticks to you:

nicotine stains from cigarettes smoked long ago

a stray herb between your teeth

the idea you can't be saved

& the ancient memory of your French teacher

reminding you to save water whilst brushing.

E.B.

It isn't enough to scroll past scoops

& watch them melt second-hand.

A flavour is only known when tasted,

& our memories are formed

through the attention we gave.

Ice Cream with my Departed Granddad

Dedicated to my maternal grandfather and Simone Weil

I thought I knew my mother:

she is a meld of her parents,

misunderstood as her grandmother

& softer within than her shell so thin,

which she inflates as psychic armour

(much like her aunt and sisters)

when she must stand her ground,

but I never saw her clearer than when

I followed a trail of her blood

to the jagged edges of my blunt words.

Interbeing

For my dear Mum and maternal ancestors

Ravens' beaks swaddle the sacred

& strut assuredly along the shore.

Never cawing their knowing

nor seek another to validate,

they have courted clear-opaque sky

of depth unknown & familiar enigma,

the shape of home & shade of bliss —

with which I'll someday merge my soul

& strut like ravens along the shore.

Gnosis

Dedicated to Michael F., whose memorial bench at Portishead seafront inspired this poem.

The One is all the pieces

we each hold a-part

& learn how to play

breaking hearts in love;

our bodies in death

releasing an anchor,

then a pen —

look back and see

it was all written:

a universe of stories.

Mosaic of Life

Life is hitched to death; I can't find a stitch to pull them apart. When asked to define truth, even language begins to eat itself.

Ouroboros

Soraya Bakhbakhi is a Welsh-Libyan poet and writer who is originally from Cardiff, the capital city of Wales. Soraya is an avid music fan who also enjoys spending time with her darling furbies. Soraya currently resides in Portishead, and its seafront is a setting which inspired many of the poems in this collection. Soraya's other interests include spirituality, consciousness, and non-human intelligence. Soraya's spiritual and life experiences have also shaped the poems in this collection.

Praise for Interbeing

Soraya explores death and spirituality with curiosity and brings compassion to what, at times, is mundane and necessary. In this authentic collection of poetry, with notes of Eastern philosophy and musical influence, Soraya has created poetry that reminds us all to "love everything anyway".

—Lindsey Heatherly, Author of
What is Home If Not A Person (Bay Media LLC, 2022)

Soraya's poems remind me of mindfulness meditations. The reverence to the past, present and future as well as a softness toward the difficult, the unpleasant or faltering are given equal grace within these lines. Reading these poems makes one stop to recognize heartbeat and breath; the heart of these poems are how they breathe life into each moment the author has so carefully witnessed and expressed.'

—K Weber, Poet and Curator of an Ongoing Series of Collaborative Poetry Collections

Soraya deftly and playfully weaves popular culture together with a kaleidoscope of spiritual and psychological teachings, into a relatable, enlightening and uplifting poetic journey.

—Polly Oliver, Poet and Author of a Forthcoming Collection from Black Bough Poetry

www.ingramcontent.com/pod-product-compliance
Lightning Source LLC
LaVergne TN
LVHW040203080526
838202LV00042B/3295